THE INDUSTRIAL REVOLUTION

Volume 7

The Worldwide Industrial Revolution

James R. Arnold & Roberta Wiener

Grolier

An imprint of Scholastic Library Publishing
Danbury, Connecticut

First published in 2005 by Grolier
An imprint of Scholastic Library Publishing
Old Sherman Turnpike
Danbury, Connecticut 06816

For information address the publisher:
Scholastic Library Publishing, Old Sherman Turnpike,
Danbury, Connecticut 06816

Library of Congress Cataloging-in-Publication Data

Arnold, James R.
    The industrial revolution / James R. Arnold and Roberta Wiener.
    p. cm
    Includes bibliographical references and index.
    Contents: v. 1. A turning point in history – v. 2. The industrial revolution begins – v. 3. The industrial revolution spreads – v. 4. The industrial revolution comes to America – v. 5. The growth of the industrial revolution in America – v. 6. The industrial revolution spreads through Europe – v. 7. The worldwide industrial revolution – v. 8. America's second industrial revolution – v. 9. The industrial revolution and the working class v. 10. The industrial revolution and American society.
    ISBN 0-7172-6031-3 (set)—ISBN 0-7172-6032-1 (v. 1)—
ISBN 0-7172-6033-X (v. 2)—ISBN 0-7172-6034-8 (v. 3)—
ISBN 0-7172-6035-6 (v. 4)—ISBN 0-7172-6036-4 (v. 5)—
ISBN 0-7172-6037-2 (v. 6)—ISBN 0-7172-6038-0 (v. 7)—
ISBN 0-7172-6039-9 (v. 8)—ISBN 0-7172-6040-2 (v. 9)—
ISBN 0-7172-6041-0 (v. 10)
    1. Industrial revolution. 2. Economic history. I. Wiener, Roberta.
II. Title.

HD2321.A73 2005
330.9'034–dc22   2004054243

Printed and bound in China

CONTENTS

INTRODUCTION

The Industrial Revolution came to Asia long after it had been firmly established in Europe and North America. Most often, western entrepreneurs and investors brought the Industrial Revolution's power-driven machinery and mechanized transport to the Far East. Even in the cases in which Asian governments took the lead, industrialization still depended heavily on the import of western technical and business methods.

The traditional peasant community in which rural people farmed and did home manufacture formed the economic basis of virtually all of Asia. Even after industrialization arrived, large-scale manufacturing remained a distinct and separate activity from the rural, peasant communities that surrounded the industrial centers. Consequently, the creation of an

Traditional agriculture persisted into the twentieth century even as Japan grew more industrialized. A twentieth-century rural laborer carrying a wooden plow on his back.

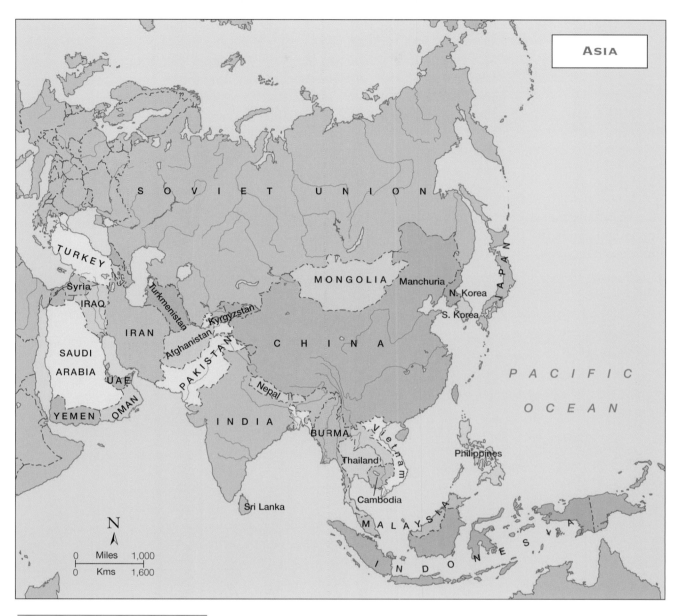

ASIA

N

| 0 | Miles | 1,000 |
| 0 | Kms | 1,600 |

Silk production, paper, waterwheels, and blast furnaces all originated in China centuries before they were seen in Europe. The cotton gin and the spinning wheel were originally seen in ancient India. Yet neither of these societies industrialized until spurred to do so by Europeans.

integrated national market, which we have seen was so essential to economic development in the West, was slow to occur.

The region that stretches from India through Southeast Asia to China and Japan contains more than half the world's population. Yet, until well after the end of World War II in 1945 this vast area made only a small contribution to the world's industrial output.

On the eve of World War II the great majority of Asian industrial activity was taking place within an exceptionally small area inside Japan and the territories Japan controlled. A few Chinese ports and coastal areas had industrialized. India had robust cotton and jute industries, although total output was about one-third of Japanese production. Elsewhere, modern manufacturing barely existed.

5

JAPAN BEGINS TO INDUSTRIALIZE

O ne hundred years after the Industrial Revolution began in England, Japan remained an isolated country governed by leaders who from the 1630s had strictly enforced a foreign policy designed to limit contact with Europeans. Almost every

FEUDAL: of the medieval system under which serfs worked on land held by a lord and gave part of their produce to the lord

Below: Commodore Matthew Perry used a display of American military might to coerce Japan into establishing diplomatic relations and trade with the United States.

year a few Dutch and Chinese ships called at Nagasaki, Japan's only open port. The government ordered a committee of samurai (members of the military class in **feudal** Japan) scholars to learn Dutch and study western books about government, science, and military matters. Otherwise, Japan remained closed to economic exchanges with western nations. This state of affairs changed dramatically in 1853, when Commodore Matthew Perry visited Japan with a powerful squadron of U.S. warships.

Perry's visit opened Japan to foreign contact and caused a social and political revolution known as the "Meiji Restoration," which overthrew the Tokugawa shoguns who had ruled Japan for 250 years (the shoguns were military

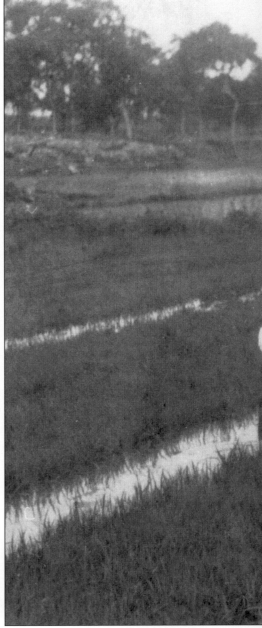

governors who controlled the country and kept the emperor from having any power). In 1868 Prince Mutsuhito became the new emperor of Japan, taking the name "Meiji" (enlightened rule). He was assisted by a government composed of former samurai.

A major Japanese goal during the Meiji period was to achieve military and material equality with the far more developed western nations. Japanese leaders understood that a large part of western superiority came from its modern industry. They resolved to develop Japanese industry in order to be able to withstand western power.

Above left: Once the United States broke Japan's longstanding isolation, the way opened for other nations to establish relations with Japan. An 1879 painting of foreign leaders who had visited Japan, including the rulers of Switzerland, Denmark, Turkey, Persia, and China.

Above: Growing rice, a staple of the Japanese diet, required intensive hand labor. Workers transplanting rice seedlings.

THE MEIJI ERA

Before Perry's visit in 1853 Japan had taken some steps toward a modern economy. Japan's agricultural sector had moved from subsistence farming to production for the market. The rise in agricultural productivity had stimulated urban economic activity. At the same time, merchants were organizing rural handicraft manufacturers into a putting-out system. Consequently, most rural villages performed some kind of manufacturing activity.

Industrial manufacture took place in the castle towns, whose leaders dominated the surrounding countryside. In

Rural girls and women stacking pottery outside a kiln.

Electric lighting:
See also
Volume 8 pages 48–51

them workers made silk and cotton textiles, pottery, and metal goods. The manufacturing processes were primitive, with no use of steam power and only modest use of water power. However, the standard of craftsmanship was high. In addition, well-established commercial organizations conducted business on behalf of the central government and feudal lords. All of this provided a basis for industrial expansion during the Meiji era.

After 1853 the manufacture of western arms particularly interested the central government and some of the provincial lords. They followed western methods and hired western experts to establish arms factories and shipyards. The armaments industry needed raw materials, so the development of mines followed. Soldiers needed uniforms, so the government built cotton-spinning mills.

Beginning with the Meiji Restoration of 1868, the government, led by an able and active group of samurai, entered into long-term planning for modernization. The new

Emperor Meiji and Empress Shoken (below) abandoned traditional Japanese dress for western clothing, demonstrating their commitment to Japan's participation in the modern world. Meiji ruled Japan until his death in 1912.

government took over existing industrial facilities and built silk factories, woolen mills, breweries, and engineering and chemical factories using western models.

For example, in the early 1870s the Meiji government introduced French silk-reeling techniques to the silk factory at Tomioka. Silk filaments had to be processed by reeling, or winding, the filaments onto a shaft and then twisting together two or more long filaments, called throwing, to make a heavier and stronger thread. Before machine power workers performed these tedious chores by hand. When the first machines came on line at the Tomioka Filature, workers, most of whom were women experienced in hand reeling, went there for training. They were then hired by private mills that installed newly imported silk-reeling machinery. The working day lasted 14 hours, but this was no more than a typical work day in a peasant household, so the laborers did not object.

Simultaneously, entrepreneurs founded important industrial firms without the aid of banks or the government. For example, Denhichi Ito owned a profitable sake (a rice-based alcoholic beverage) company. He anticipated opportunity in cotton textiles and used his own and his family's savings to invest in a cotton mill. When the investment boom in the cotton textile industry began in 1875, Ito was already well positioned to benefit. His firm grew into one of the largest in Japan.

Private initiative also launched the Tokyo Electric Light Company. A physics student at the University of Tokyo convinced eight wealthy merchants of the merit of having electric light in Japan. After gaining a charter in 1882, the merchants struggled for four years to overcome investors' deep skepticism about this novel business. Most bankers had never seen an electric light and were understandably reluctant to invest. Finally the company became established, and the public enthusiastically purchased shares.

Twentieth-century rural Japanese worker hand-reeling silk off the cocoons of silkworms.

In the absence of banking assistance entrepreneurs during the early Meiji period relied on their own optimism about the potential benefits of industrialization to self-finance new industrial firms.

Gradually the Meiji government built the necessary infrastructure for industrialization beginning with a sound currency and a modern banking system. Later it established a telegraph and postal system, railway and shipping services, and a general and technical education system. By 1885 the Meiji government had overcome large deficits and made other necessary reforms to create economic conditions to support industrial growth. The next 15 years witnessed Japan's first great wave of industrial investment.

Japan hosted an industrial exposition (right) in 1881.

Silk:
See also
Volume 1 page 35
Volume 6 page 25

Nonetheless, for the remainder of the century Japan had a mix of modern and primitive industry. For example, some weaving factories operated power looms, but home manufacturers using hand looms still produced most of the nation's cloth. Likewise the traditional silk industry saw a fourfold expansion in the production of raw silk, yet power-driven machinery made less than half of the total output, with peasants, working in small mills or at home, hand reeling the balance.

By 1890 very little heavy industry existed. Government factories and a few private enterprises made chemicals, glass, and cement. Western techniques had been introduced to the coal, copper, and oil industries, yet output remained small.

THE ZAIBATSU

The zaibatsu ("wealthy clique" or "money group" in Japanese) were a uniquely Japanese form of capitalist enterprise. The zaibatsu formed after the Meiji Restoration in 1868 in response to the national drive toward modernization. They were somewhat like the cartels or trusts that arose in the west but were usually organized around a single family. Some of the families had been prominent since feudal times; others came to prominence by grasping the opportunities presented by a new era. The four main zaibatsu were Mitsui, Mitsubushi, Sumitomo, and Yasuda.

Many of Japan's political leaders formed close ties with specific families. The government needed those business families to carry out its industrial policy because the zaibatsu possessed scarce technical knowledge and capital. The zaibatsu underwrote government loans and entered into new businesses that the government thought desirable. In return, the government sold the zaibatsu state properties at low prices and granted them favorable contracts.

Right: During the early 1900s textile mills employed close to 60 percent of all Japanese industrial workers. Eighty percent were women, and 60 percent were under the age of 20. Women operating silk-reeling machinery.

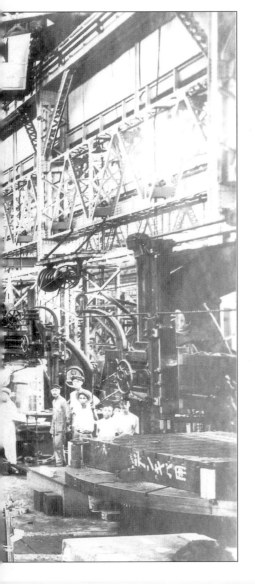

Left: Machine shop at the Mitsubishi plant around 1925.

Consequently, the zaibatsu operated in nearly all important economic sectors by owning or having large investments in companies engaged in important activities such as textile manufacture, mining, food processing, and machinery. To secure capital to invest in industry, the zaibatsu owned banks, and most were active in foreign trade as well.

The absence of western competitors during World War I (1914-1918) gave the zaibatsu a great opportunity to expand and conquer foreign markets in Asia. During the interwar period the zaibatsu closely cooperated with Imperial Japan's aggressive military expansion in Asia. Consequently, the Allied occupation authorities who controlled Japan after its defeat in 1945 ordered the zaibatsu dissolved.

However, the management of individual companies did not noticeably change, and many companies continued to loosely cooperate just as they had always done. The cooperation among leading companies and banks, a legacy of the zaibatsu, became a central factor in propelling Japan's tremendous economic growth after World War II. In the modern world some of the names of the original zaibatsu are associated with world-recognized brand names such as Mitsubishi automobiles.

Iron production was insignificant. The ship-building industry only made small vessels for the coasting trade.

Although Japan was not yet a significant industrial nation, it had made very rapid progress in a short amount of time. It had made the changes necessary to create a modern industrial society. Most importantly, the great business houses, the zaibatsu, had become firmly established. They were to influence heavily and eventually dominate Japanese industrial development.

THE DORMITORY GIRLS

After 1895 the pace of industrialization accelerated dramatically.

Even in the twentieth century many Japanese laborers transported their produce to market on open boats propelled by men using poles.

Just as had occurred elsewhere, the textile industry led the way. Between 1893 and 1913 cotton yarn output increased from 90 million pounds to more than 600 million. Cotton spinning became Japan's greatest industry, with 80 percent of the mills located in Osaka.

Textile mills competed to hire workers. The competition was so intense that the mills guarded their workers to prevent them from leaving for employment somewhere else. Middlemen procured workers and generally sought unsophisticated peasant girls from poverty-stricken regions because they were easiest to fool by making false promises about employment at a textile mill. Young female workers, recruited from rural

areas, provided a tractable, cheap labor force for the new mills. They made up 62 percent of the factory labor force in 1907.

The textile mills operated in two twelve-hour shifts. After completing a shift, the girls went to a dormitory room that merely consisted of an open floor covered with sleeping mattresses, with each girl assigned to a three-by-six-foot mattress. They were forbidden to walk outside the dormitory until they had proven their loyalty to the company. Likewise, leaving the dormitory on a holiday or a Sunday was a special privilege given to loyal workers only. Guards kept close watch to prevent desertion. Deserters received physical punishment, including beatings. This prisonlike life lasted for fixed terms of employment of three to five years.

Forced labor:
See also
Volume 9 pages 46–47

The ruthless exploitation of labor helped the cotton mills generate profit. Then, having mastered modern manufacturing techniques, Japanese businessmen turned to opportunities in China and in Korea. By 1900 Japan had captured the cotton market in those countries.

FURTHER INDUSTRIAL GROWTH

To avoid dependence on foreign supplies, the government worked hard at developing its metal industries. Although they lacked raw materials such as coking coal, their determination led to the construction of great iron and steel works. Still, by 1913 iron and steel production fell far short of the country's needs.

Western battleships dwarf Japanese sailboats in Yokohama harbor during the 1870s. A small passenger train in the foreground represents the extent of Japan's railroad development at the time.

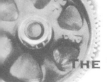

Factories in Tokyo's industrial district around 1920.

The government had built Japan's first railway—only 17 miles of track—in 1875 and after that left it to private enterprise to develop the rail system. By 1913 a fine rail system was in place, with about 7,000 miles of track. Government subsidies and special benefits helped the Japanese merchant fleet to expand dramatically so that they carried about half of all imports and exports. Likewise, government initiatives inspired the creation of numerous heavy industries, including rubber and sugar refining, fertilizer, cement, paper, and glass. Once they were created, the zaibatsu took over the day-to-day running of those industries.

Although compared to western nations Japan remained primarily a rural, agriculture-based country, by the beginning of World War I its industry was well ahead of other Asian countries. A few characteristics had emerged, including a tendency toward monopoly control of industry in the form of the zaibatsu and a strong resistance to unionization.

THE BOXER REBELLION

A popular uprising supported by the Chinese government sought to eject all foreigners from China. Foreigners named it the "Boxer Rebellion" because it was led by a secret society that practiced ritual exercises resembling boxing.

Housing for Tokyo's industrial workers.

The first significant trade union in Japanese labor history was the Metalworkers Union organized in Tokyo in 1897. Police harassment was constant, and in 1900 the government passed a law, the "Public Peace Police Law," that effectively ended union activity. In conflicts between employers and workers the employers held all the advantages until 1911 and the passage of Japan's first Factory Law, which provided for better working conditions.

In 1914 Japan stood well poised to take advantage of the opportunities presented by World War I. In the absence of western competitors Japan experienced a strong Asian demand for its goods and services, and that stimulated a tremendous expansion in Japanese industrial activity. By 1929, just 61 years after the beginning of the Meiji Dynasty, Japan had vaulted into the ranks of the world's industrial powers.

THE INDUSTRIAL REVOLUTION IN CHINA

Around the time the Industrial Revolution began in England, China had a widely admired manufacturing sector. European traders who operated through the Chinese port of Canton found that Chinese merchants had no interest in goods manufactured in Europe because they were of insufficient quality. On the other hand, European consumers coveted excellent Chinese silk and cotton goods as well as Chinese porcelain. What few appreciated was that those Chinese goods were made by skilled craftsmen without benefit of power machinery. China proved to be a "latecomer" to the Industrial Revolution, lagging behind Japan by about 25 years, and not getting started on the path to industrialization until after 1890.

China exhibited porcelain, enameled goods, silks, and paper at the 1876 Centennial Exposition in Philadelphia.

Market stalls along a street in Canton, China, during the 1880s.

CHINESE RESISTANCE TO WESTERN IDEAS

While Japanese leaders sought to overcome Japan's technical inferiority by launching a vigorous effort to industrialize, Chinese leaders were contemptuous of all aspects of western civilization. In their minds westerners were intruders, mere barbarians (an attitude they shared with the Japanese) with nothing important to offer to China's superior culture. Furthermore, the Chinese ruling class, unlike Japanese leaders, was not interested in directing social and economic change.

The few Chinese leaders who tried to promote industrialization found that they could make little progress against the traditional, deeply conservative leadership.

Consequently, it was left to westerners, acting out of self-interest, to take the lead in promoting Chinese industrialization.

EUROPEANS TAKE THE LEAD

After 1842, by virtue of their superior military might, Europeans had forced China to open several ports in addition to Canton. In those places, called the Concessions, Europeans could settle and trade, but the Chinese government severely restricted most economic activities. Outside of their coastal enclaves Europeans encountered legal obstacles to any effort to promote industrialization. For example, British entrepreneurs built a railroad connecting two ports in 1876. Chinese authorities did not like it, purchased the property, and destroyed it!

Within the Concessions Europeans utilized modern methods to process Chinese commodities for the export market. They established steam-powered silk mills and factories for pressing tea into bricks so the tea could be better stored aboard merchant ships. Europeans set up machinery to

A traditional Chinese tea merchant's shop.

process straw braid and bristles for brushes, and to extract oil from beans. Around 1850 Europeans built shipyards in Shanghai to repair vessels that participated in the Chinese trade. By western standards all of these industrial facilities operated on a small scale.

Canton, an ancient port city, had conducted tightly restricted trade with Europeans since 1699. Angered by the trade limitations, Great Britain fought a war with China from 1839 to 1842. The victorious Britons imposed the following conditions: China had to give Hong Kong to the British and open Canton, Shanghai, and three other ports to unrestricted trade. France and the United States quickly insisted on the same access.

Outside the factories people transported goods without the aid of machinery. Chinese laborers carrying crates of tea.

A New Era Begins

In 1895 Japan and China concluded a war with a treaty that gave Japan the right to engage in manufacture in specified ports. Because of a "most-favored-nation" clause in China's treaties with European powers, what Japan could do (Japan being the most-favored nation) the European nations could also do. Later, following the resolution of the Boxer Rebellion in 1901, those rights expanded to include the ability to participate in mining activities inside China. Because of those changes the Industrial Revolution finally came to China on a meaningful scale.

Western capitalists and Chinese entrepreneurs established cotton mills. By 1900 China had 570,000 power-driven spindles in operation. In 1913 the number had more than doubled to 1.2 million. Mechanization came to the silk industry. An association of British and Chinese investors formed to bring modern methods to the coal-mining industry.

However, China was a huge country, and it lacked an efficient transport system: This lack seriously impeded

Unloading bales of cotton at a waterfront Shanghai cotton mill around 1890.

A popular uprising supported by the Chinese government sought to eject all foreigners from China. Foreigners named it the "Boxer Rebellion" because it was led by a secret society that practiced ritual exercises resembling boxing.

A Chinese laborer carrying 200 pounds of raw cotton to a Shanghai factory in 1924.

The railroad came to Manchuria, but most people continued to rely on such age-old modes of transportation as the horse cart.

Above: The luxurious interior of an early passenger rail car in Manchuria.

Below: A Russian-built locomotive in Manchuria.

industrialization. The Chinese government understood that railroad construction required enormous sums, and that they would have to use foreign investors. The government feared that if it permitted such investment, it would lose political control to foreigners. Nonetheless, around 1900 the Russians received permission to build "a concession line" in Manchuria (a part of China bordering the Russian empire), and this began China's railroad era. Other foreign nations as well as the Chinese government itself sponsored enough construction projects so that by 1913 rail lines connected most major Chinese cities.

China's path to industrialization was unique. In 1913 it ranked in the top six manufacturing nations in the world in terms of total output. Most of that output came from older industries, particularly textiles. China did not experience the rapid technological changes occurring in the west in the steel, chemical, electrical engineering, and automobile industries. Furthermore, until 1937 foreign firms owned almost all of its large industrial establishments. While other nations had brought native enterprise to bear in their drive toward industrialization, China did not. After World War I a new government actively planned to extend the railroads and expand industry. But conflict with Japan followed by civil war wrecked China's industrial prospects.

Modern industrialization did not take firm hold in China until after the Communist government took power following World War II. In many ways the Chinese Industrial Revolution is still taking place.

INDUSTRIALIZATION IN INDIA

Spinning fine yarn

India's economic position in 1800 was similar to that of China and Japan. The great majority of the population lived in rural areas and supported themselves by farming. Peasants worked at various cottage industries to supplement their incomes. In certain regions skilled craftsmen made luxury goods for sale to the wealthy. Foreigners, including Europeans, considered Indian cotton a desirable commodity. A British admirer wrote in 1835, "The Indians have in all ages maintained an unapproached and almost incredible perfection in their fabrics of cotton. Some of their muslins might be thought the work of fairies, or of insects, rather than of men."

Warping

OBSTACLES TO INDUSTRIALIZATION

When the west began to produce machine-made textiles, those textiles took over much of the market for Indian cotton and contributed to a gradual decay of Indian cottage industry. The decline accelerated once the railroad era in India began. Rail lines

Reeling yarn from a reed

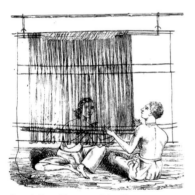

Applying the reed to the warp

Weaving

Forming the heddles

Indians making muslins in 1866, a few years after the British took over India. The expansion of the British Empire brought British textile goods to the less developed world. As fine as India muslins were, native cottage industry could not compete with cheaper, mass-produced British textiles.

Steaming cloths during the process of bleaching

Arranging displaced threads in cloth

connected the interior with major ports, exposing traditional Indian textiles to western imports. Hand-made textiles could not effectively compete with machine manufacture.

Most importantly, conditions in India were less favorable to the creation of new industries than in countries such as Japan. The United Kingdom took over direct rule of India in 1858. The British in India naturally represented British interests over Indian interests. Unlike the nationalist government of Japan, which promoted modernization to resist foreign aggression, the British-controlled Indian government had no such motive. Furthermore, the United Kingdom held the view that governments should not participate directly in manufacturing. Consequently, there was no government impetus for industrialization.

Finally, Indian social traditions and institutions did not encourage large-scale industry. The Indian caste system (its unique class structure) defined permissible jobs for members at each level. The upper and middle classes simply would not consider participating in a wide range of economic activities.

NINETEENTH-CENTURY INDUSTRIAL DEVELOPMENT

The year 1853 saw the completion of India's first rail line. After that construction went on at a steady pace, with 25,000 miles in service by 1900 and 35,000 by 1914. Railroad construction led to the expansion of the coal industry both by

By 1895 rail lines extended well beyond India's major cities.

Indian workers building railroad cars in 1895.

increasing demand for coal and by linking major coal-mining regions with industrial and commercial centers. Coal production increased sufficiently so that by 1900 India switched from a net importer to a net exporter of coal. Still, compared both to the size of its population and to production figures in leading industrial nations, Indian coal production was small.

The only two factory industries that developed significantly during the nineteenth century were the cotton and jute industries (jute is a fibrous plant used to make burlap and rope). A modern cotton-spinning mill had been established in Bombay in 1853, but little additional industrial development occurred until railroads linked Bombay with the cotton-growing regions of the interior. After railroad links were established in 1880, the cotton industry in Bombay took off and spread to other parts of India. By 1900 India had become the world's fourth leading producer of cotton yarn.

The completion of important rail links likewise caused the Indian jute industry to experience similar growth. Before the railroads India had exported a considerable amount of raw jute to Dundee, Scotland, for finishing. After the necessary rail links were in place, Scottish capitalists imported British machinery into India and installed it in jute-spinning and -weaving mills. Mechanization proved so successful that by

1908 Indian mills manufactured more jute than mills in Dundee. However, industrial success came at the cost of destroying the old Indian jute industry.

EARLY TWENTIETH-CENTURY INDUSTRIAL GROWTH

Before 1913 the development of new industries or the mechanization of traditional industries was limited to textiles and mining along with some iron and steel production. Also, a small engineering sector had emerged to service equipment used in mining, railroading, and textile manufacturing. Census statistics for 1911 underscore the concentration of industry within a small range. Among establishments that employed 20 or more people, factories and mines had 1,150,000 workers. Almost 50 percent of those factory and mine workers labored in textile industries, with the great majority employed in cotton spinning and jute manufacture. Another 20 percent worked in mines. In other words, only three industries employed about 70 percent of all industrial workers.

As in China, in 1913 India's high ranking among the world's leading manufacturing nations resulted from the output of

A modern twentieth-century cotton mill in Bombay.

older industries, primarily textiles. Also like China, India did not experience the rapid technological changes taking place in the west such as innovations in steel making and the introduction of new products in the chemical or electrical engineering industries.

After World War I British policy toward Indian industrial development changed. Instead of taking a hands-off approach in keeping with traditional British economic philosophy, an Industrial Commission recommended in 1918 that: "the government must play an active part in the industrial development of the country." In response, the government set protective tariffs to allow new industries to emerge. From that time on Indian industrial activity expanded, although it still remained small by European standards until recent times.

The Industrial Revolution came to India in the absence of government encouragement. Although capitalists had the freedom to invest in mechanization, by and large they chose not to. The lack of positive government encouragement was a decisive factor in limiting Indian industrial development until at least 1918.

Indian laborers unloading bales of jute from river boats in 1895.

INDUSTRIAL GROWTH IN SOUTHEAST ASIA

Industrial development in Southeast Asia was limited to specific areas in what is today Malaysia and Indonesia, and came almost entirely from mining. Both were colonial territories, with the British gradually replacing the Portuguese and Dutch in control of Malaysia, while the Dutch retained control of Indonesia.

THE TIN-MINING INDUSTRY

In both Indonesia and Malaysia tin was the major mining product. In Malaysia the native peoples had mined tin before

Chinese tin miners at work in Indonesia, using American-made drills.

the arrival of Europeans at the beginning of the sixteenth century. Tin mining continued at a modest level until around 1850, when new, rich ore resources were discovered.

Immigrant Chinese entrepreneurs directed most of the tin industry until 1913. Between 1850 and 1913 the output of tin concentrates (the product of tin smelting) increased more than sevenfold. After that, European capitalists introduced new mining techniques that required specialized technical knowledge and large capital resources. By 1929 the output of European-owned mines equaled that of Chinese-owned mines.

From 1900 on, Chinese entrepreneurs were also active in starting small-scale manufacturing for local consumption. Chinese-owned facilities made products ranging from biscuits to cement. However, apart from tin smelters and one engineering machine shop, Malaysia had no modern, large-scale industry until the 1930s.

Although in Malaysia the British government encouraged foreign investment and operational control, the situation was different in Indonesia. There the Dutch colonial government controlled tin mining by completely owning one of the two large mining companies and partially owning the other. As explored in Volume 6, that was in keeping with the Dutch policy of organizing the economies of the so-called Dutch East Indies entirely for their own benefit.

The colonial Dutch government operated a few smelting facilities in Indonesia but usually preferred to ship tin to Singapore for smelting. The discovery of large oil resources, particularly in Borneo, did little to change the pattern in which the Dutch government ran its colony for its own benefit.

Large-scale manufacture did not make a significant contribution to the economies of either Malaysia or Indonesia until 1930. The worldwide depression caused both countries to begin their own manufacturing operations to make products that formerly had been imported. Industrial activities continued to be centered around mining and, in the case of Indonesia, oil extraction and refining. After World War II the Industrial Revolution arrived in Southeast Asia in full force with the construction of modern factories in Malaysia and on Singapore Island. In Indonesia, however, the political turmoil associated with independence from the Netherlands hampered industrial development.

FAR EAST SUMMARY

The scale of industrial development in Japan, China, India, Malaysia, and Indonesia was uneven. Likewise, each of those five countries developed industries for different reasons. In

Cotton mills in Shanghai, one of China's coastal enclaves where westerners dominated economic life.

Japan native determination by both the government and private entrepreneurs was the most significant cause of industrial achievement. China, in contrast, resisted change and limited foreign involvement as best it could. The industrialization that occurred took place within the coastal enclaves dominated by westerners.

India, Malaysia, and Indonesia were all colonies. The British government did not actively encourage industrial development in India, though it did provide a stable political and legal environment that should have been favorable to such development. Yet industrialization barely occurred and came mostly from foreign entrepreneurs.

In Malaysia, like India, the British government did not participate directly in industrial development. In contrast, the Dutch government firmly controlled development in Indonesia. In both countries the leadership for innovation came from outside, and in both countries the immigrant Chinese made outstanding contributions.

THE INDUSTRIAL REVOLUTION IN LATIN AMERICA

Between 1850 and the outbreak of World War I in 1914 a tremendous economic expansion occurred. Western and central Europe and the United States had the world's most productive manufacturing methods based on widespread use of industrial machinery. The rest of the world concentrated its economic efforts on the production of foodstuffs and raw materials. They traded those items for manufactured goods produced in the more industrialized nations. The colonial economies, as most were called, exported products that they had harvested, gathered, or mined from the earth. Those exports were usually in their raw state or were only slightly processed to reduce bulk and weight for shipping. Only limited

Young women working in a Mexican factory in 1903 make burlap bags used to pack coffee beans for shipment.

and scattered industrial activity took place within the colonial economies.

THE EXPORT ECONOMY

The leaders of Central and South America overwhelmingly descended from Spanish or Portuguese colonists. During colonial times these economic and political leaders focused on

Left: Cane-cutting machines at a Cuban sugar cane mill around 1920.

Below: Harvesting sugar cane on a Cuban plantation in 1904.

the production and export of commodities such as sugar and coffee. A very small portion of those goods was consumed within Latin America.

In addition, many Central and South American nations depended heavily on only one or two raw products. In 1938 sugar made up 70 percent of Cuba's total exports. Bolivia, with its tin, and Panama, with its bananas, were in similar situations. Copper and nitrates (for fertilizers) accounted for two-thirds of the value of Chile's exports. Venezuela, with its petroleum, and El Salvador, with its coffee, were even more dependent (90 percent of total value) on a single item for exports.

One consequence of such heavy dependence on a single thing was that a significant decline in exports, whether caused by domestic crop failure or international change in demand, always caused serious economic problems and often political disruptions. Such economic and political disruptions impeded industrialization and economic growth.

A tin mining facility in Bolivia, showing worker housing in the background.

Early in the twentieth century some Ecuadorian banana growers sent their produce to market on river rafts.

Another factor restricting development was dependence on foreign investment to finance industrialization. The flow of capital from the industrialized nations to Latin America was erratic. It rose and fell based on economic conditions outside of Latin America and sometimes ceased entirely for years at a time. Moreover, declining exports usually occurred simultaneously with declining foreign investment. In other words, markets for exports and sources of new investment

A foreign-owned copper mining complex in Chile.

dried up at the same time, causing economic depression and setbacks to industrialization.

Before the Great Depression of the 1930s few people understood the importance for Latin America of foreign markets and foreign investment. Even earlier few Latin Americans were aware of the problems caused by the region's failure to experience the rising living standards brought by the Industrial Revolution.

41

Left: A Chilean plant for production of nitrates, used as fertilizer.

Below: A Central American coffee plantation; transplanting seedlings (opposite top); protective coverings for the plants (opposite center); and mature coffee trees (opposite below).

Only the wealthy elite who had descended from European colonists enjoyed increased prosperity. They controlled large-scale farming and the harvesting and mining of raw materials. They alone benefitted from the increasing amounts of Latin American exports consumed by the industrialized world. Meanwhile, the vast majority of native peoples lived in poverty and permanent poor health, and survived by subsistence farming.

A wide gap exists between the living conditions of the rich and poor in Latin America. A mansion in a South American city.

Below right: Worker's houses on an Ecuadorian plantation in 1907.

Bottom: Latin America's subsistence farmers survived on what they could grow to feed themselves plus whatever money they could earn selling surplus produce at local markets.

The suffering caused by the Great Depression of the 1930s taught Latin American leaders the danger of an economy that relies so heavily on the export of a single commodity. Since that time many have tried to diversify their economies, and part of that diversification has involved industrialization.

Because of a unique set of circumstances related to their colonial origins, the nations of Latin America have lagged far behind in industrialization. For many of them the Industrial

SOUTH AMERICA

European explorers from Spain and Portugal first set foot on South American soil in the early 1500s, and the two nations soon came to dominate the continent. Three hundred years later South Americans began fighting for and gaining their independence.

Revolution came after the end of World War II in 1945 and has continued into recent times.

WORLD OVERVIEW

In spite of World War I, living standards among the industrialized countries rose. In contrast, colonial economies experienced little improvement and remained largely without industry. After World War I, and particularly after World War II, many newly independent nations concluded that industrialization was the key to higher standards of living. Furthermore, once former colonies gained independence, their new and strongly felt nationalism motivated them to achieve economic independence through industrialization as a means to protect their political independence.

NEW TECHNOLOGIES IN THE WEST

The speed of the diffusion, or spread, of the Industrial Revolution from England through Europe and Asia depended on unique circumstances among the latecomers. But even while the first English-inspired innovations and inventions appeared in distant nations, technology in the birthplace of the Industrial Revolution and among the "first comers" did not stand still.

The earliest factory steam engines generated only about 6 horsepower. The 70-foot-tall, 700-ton Corliss steam engine featured as the centerpiece of the 1876 Centennial Exposition in Philadelphia generated some 1,500 horsepower. By means of drive shafts extending up the aisles, the engine powered all the machinery in the machine exhibit hall, running nonstop for 6 months. George Corliss, an American engineer and inventor, designed and built the engine.

TOWARD MORE POWERFUL ENGINES

Watt's steam engine (see Volume 2) had launched a revolution in how humankind used energy. As time passed, technicians made impressive improvements on Watt's design by working with higher pressures and compound expansion (multiple expansions of the gas in the cylinder to extract the maximum amount of energy from the steam). Between 1850 and 1900 machine pressures increased by a factor of four or five, while triple and even quadruple expansion engines were developed. However, by the end of the 1800s most of the improvements possible had been made. Meanwhile, new industrial processes required greater power. It was impractical to build steam engines on the colossal scale necessary to generate such power.

The obvious way to obtain more power was to run the engine faster. But technical limitations related to conversion of reciprocating (back-and-forth) to rotary (circular) motion limited engine speed. Quite simply, the stresses generated by high-speed operation led to engine breakdown. The development of the steam turbine overcame this technical limitation.

Water driven-turbines dated back to 1827 (see Volume 3). In a water turbine the force of flowing water pushed vanes on a wheel to produce rotary motion. While more efficient than traditional waterwheels, water turbines were only useful at selected sites where the water flow was sufficient. What

An outward-flow water turbine of the sort used to run American textile mills during the 1850s. Water dropped into the center of the turbine and turned the vanes as it flowed out. This turbine could generate up to 650 horsepower.

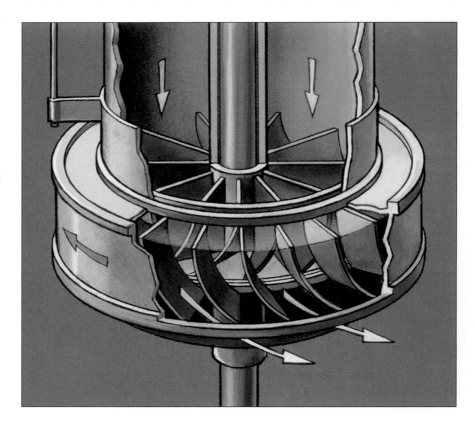

industry needed was a means to obtain power that was not shackled to flowing water. It took until 1884 for the English engineer Charles Parsons to develop a practical steam turbine. Instead of using steam pressure as in a traditional steam engine, the Parsons machine used the kinetic energy of moving steam to push curved blades attached to a wheel. The rotation of the wheel generated electricity.

The Parsons machine was more powerful than any motor of its time. To accompany it, Parsons also developed a **generator** that exceeded all previous designs. His turbine and generator were the most significant innovations since Watt's engine. The steam turbine was smaller, lighter, and cheaper to build than a steam engine. In 1887 the modern era of steam turbine electricity generation began when the Fourth Banks Power Station at Newcastle-upon-Tyne in England installed four Parsons engines. The steam turbine soon became the preferred technology to generate power throughout the world. It made possible the later development of a large-scale electrical power industry.

GENERATOR: an engine that converts mechanical energy, such as flowing water, to electrical energy

THE AGE OF STEEL

Compared to any other metal, iron had an incomparable combination of advantages: great strength in proportion to weight and volume, plasticity (the ability to be molded or shaped), and hardness. Iron was exceptionally strong compared to other metals. It had good plasticity, meaning it could be shaped without significant loss of elasticity, and hammered, cut, stamped, drilled, filed, ground, melted, and cast. Iron allowed precise, clean cuts and the boring of smooth holes. It held its shape well in heat and withstood wear. From the earliest days of the Industrial Revolution craftsmen depended on iron for the most important parts of a machine. As soon as mass-produced iron became available and affordable, they made entire machines out of iron.

The higher the **carbon** content, the harder the metal. Less carbon made metal softer, more malleable (and thus easier to hammer), and more ductile (thus easier to draw into wires). Carbon content distinguished steel (0.1 to about 2 percent carbon) from softer wrought iron (carbon content less than 0.1 percent) and harder pig iron (carbon content 2.5 to 4 percent). Each form of iron had its uses and its drawbacks. Wrought iron could be worked by hand but did not withstand shock and wore quickly. Pig iron was hard but brittle, useful for pots and pans as well as engine blocks but unable to withstand stress.

CARBON: a chemical element found in all organic compounds and many inorganic compounds

Steel combined the advantages of both. Craftsmen ground steel to a sharp edge with the knowledge that the edge would last. This made steel useful for everything from household

knives to machine tools for cutting and shaping other metals. But on the eve of the Industrial Revolution making steel was very expensive, so steel was used only for small, high-value objects like razors, surgical tools, blades, and files.

Benjamin Huntsman's invention for making **crucible** steel (1740 to 1742, see Volume 2) produced a purer and harder metal. The first crucibles were only 9 to 11 inches tall. A hundred years later they were still only about 16 inches tall and held around 50 pounds of metal. In order to manufacture large pieces, hundreds of crucibles had to be poured as fast as possible to produce ingots weighing several tons. Because it was so labor intensive, crucible steel remained expensive. The one large crucible steel product that could always find a market regardless of expense was a steel artillery piece for the military.

Because steel was so superior to wrought iron, technicians spent considerable time and money to discover a cheap steel-manufacturing process. Henry Cort (see Volume 2) had invented a process whereby hot, liquid iron was stirred, or puddled, to draw the impurities to the surface. In the early

CRUCIBLE: a container, treated to withstand extreme heat, used for melting a material such as metal

The crucible process spread throughout the world. American metal workers using small crucibles in 1904.

The German steel firm Krupp created a sensation at the 1851 Crystal Palace Exhibition in London, England, when it displayed a 2.25-ton steel cylinder manufactured by the crucible process. In 1876 Krupp displayed a cannon at the 1876 Centennial Exposition in Philadelphia.

1840s a pair of German technicians took the next step toward using puddling to make steel. They tackled the challenge of stopping the puddling process while enough carbon remained in the liquid metal to make steel. It was hard to detect when the steel was ready. The temperature had to be kept high enough to melt the pig iron and low enough to let the steel separate out as a pasty mass.

The German puddling process produced steel that was cheaper, although of lower quality, than crucible steel. By the 1850s the most up-to-date continental producers, particularly in Germany and France, employed this process to make giant wheels, gears, and drive shafts.

HENRY BESSEMER

Often solutions to vexing technical problems turn out to be very simple, and people are amazed that someone did not think of them earlier. Such was the case with an inspiration that led to mass-produced steel.

Steel became the material of choice to make the gears and drive shafts that transferred power generated by turbines or engines to industrial machinery.

Below: Sir Henry Bessemer unveiled his new steelmaking process in 1856. The first Bessemer forge began operating in the United States in 1864 in Troy, New York. In 1873 Bethlehem Steel in Pennsylvania became the first company to mass-produce Bessemer steel.

HEMATITE: a type of iron ore valued for its high iron content; its name comes from the Greek word for blood because of its reddish color

Pig iron had always been heated around its edges. In 1851 a Kentucky iron master, William Kelly, invented a process for converting pig iron into steel. Across the Atlantic, and during the same period, the British inventor Henry Bessemer devised a similar method to blow air into and through the molten metal to remove the carbon while using the heat of the reaction to keep the iron liquid. Bessemer's converter, as it became known, was a huge increase in energy efficiency: It removed carbon from three to five tons of pig iron in 10 to 20 minutes instead of the 24 hours required by former approaches. For the first time in history steel produced in a Bessemer converter could compete on a price basis with wrought iron.

The major technical obstacle confronting Bessemer's process related to the presence of impurities, particularly phosphorus, in the pig iron. Bessemer had been lucky that he had been working with a pure form of pig iron. But even small quantities of phosphorus made steel unworkable when using his process. When Bessemer learned about this problem, he said it came "as a bolt from the blue."

Hematite ores (ores without phosphorus) existed in only a few known locations. Great Britain had a major field, Spain had the richest hematite bed in Europe, and about half of the Lake Superior basin (the Mesabi Range) in the United States contained this valuable ore. The limited supply of hematite ore restricted the spread of the Bessemer process.

An advanced design combined air pockets and bricks to allow a furnace to hold a high temperature for a long period of time.

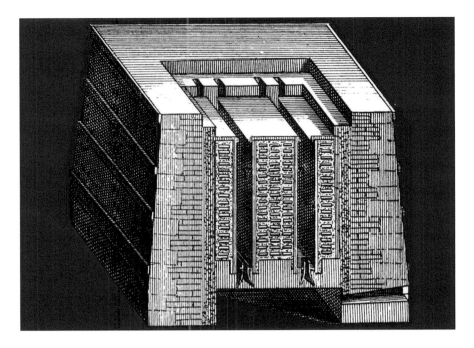

Below: Rail cars carried valuable hematite ore from the Mesabi Range to Duluth, Minnesota, a port on Lake Superior. The ore then traveled by barge across the lake.

TOWARD MASS-PRODUCED STEEL

A second major technical advance, the Siemens-Martin process (named for two German brothers, Frederick and William Siemens, and Pierre Martin) also contributed to mass-produced steel. The Siemens brothers invented a type of furnace, the open hearth furnace, that used the waste gases generated during the heating of the pig iron to warm a honeycomb of bricks. The bricks, in turn, superheated the air and gas to achieve a far higher furnace temperature, which made it possible to remove more impurities from iron. Furthermore, a separate unit generated the gas, allowing the burning of cheap, low-grade coal.

Commercial success did not come until 1864, when Martin introduced scrap iron into the hot bath in order to remove carbon. Technicians had to use trial and error to arrive at how much scrap iron to add to the bath. Each manufacturer used different grades of ore, iron, and coal, so there was no one right answer. Nonetheless, by the early 1870s most technical problems had been solved, and the age of steel began.

Great Britain, with its domestic source of hematite ore, held a great strategic advantage over its continental rivals France and Germany. Then two Englishmen, Sidney Gilchrist Thomas, a police court clerk, and his cousin Percy Gilchrist, a chemist in a Welsh iron works, made a discovery that again changed the steel industry.

Thomas was a gifted tinkerer like many of the other inventors and innovators who advanced the Industrial Revolution. He approached the problem of phosphorus contamination, a problem that some of Europe's most highly trained engineers had been unable to solve, with an open mind.

Thomas and his chemist cousin added basic limestone into the molten iron to draw off the phosphorus in a slag, or waste product. This was well-known, simple chemistry. The cousins' innovation was to line the Bessemer converter with chemically basic material instead of the usual acidic bricks in order to prevent the slag from eating away the walls of the converter and releasing the phosphorus from the slag back into the metal. This approach, called basic (a chemical term, the opposite of acidic) steel, ensured that the phosphorus came out of the converter while safely trapped by chemical bonds to the slag.

The world literally beat a path to Thomas's door to ask to lease his patent. Supposedly, two leading German steel manufacturers raced to Thomas's home to be the first to obtain

Steel:
See also
Volume 2 pages 35–40
Volume 8 pages 52–57

A 40-ton basic open hearth furnace, in use in the United States by the late 1880s.

permission, and the one who did not stop for sleep won! The commercial manufacture of basic steel began in 1879. Four years later western and central Europe had 84 Bessemer converters with a capacity of 755 tons.

Three new processes—the Bessemer converter, the Siemens-Martin open hearth, and Thomas's basic steel—reduced the cost of crude steel by 80 to 90 percent between 1860 and 1895. From 1861, before the Bessemer process gained commercial acceptance, to 1913 the combined steel production of the United Kingdom, France, Belgium, and Germany increased by a factor of 83.

Steel took over the metal-using world. Bessemer steel was cheaper, less uniform in quality, and mostly used to make rails. Steel railway rails lasted six times longer than iron. Siemens-Martin steel was more expensive, more uniform in quality, and best suited to make plates. The world's largest ship builder,

Bessemer steel rails represented a great advance for railways.

Great Britain, employed this process to build steel ships that had the advantage over iron ships of being lighter, faster, and stronger, and thus able to carry more cargo. Steel also provided the structural strength to build towering buildings called "skyscrapers" that literally changed the skyline of major urban areas worldwide.

Mechanization swept the steel-making industry. Mechanical loaders fed the raw materials into the flames of huge, tiltable furnaces equipped with **hydraulic** or electric controls. The steel then was mechanically moved to rolling mills for shaping. The most efficient facilities performed all of this work under one roof. But many countries, and Great Britain in particular, had invested fortunes in the older processes. Conservative British and French manufacturers clung to the old ways and fell behind in the industrial race.

So it was that among all European nations Germany led the way by building steel mills that were large, efficient, and integrated—meaning many processes from blast furnace to rolling mill were located in the same plant. Although at the start of the Industrial Revolution European visitors had come to Wedgwood's pottery works (see Volume 2) and British iron mills to see the best industrial practices, by the dawn of the twentieth century the situation was reversed. British visitors came to German steel mills to marvel at the efficient German use of fuel, the placement of bins to catch oil from the lubrication boxes, the recycling of spent steam.

The superiority of German steel became painfully apparent when World War I began, and German warships proved structurally superior to those of the Royal Navy.

German industry:
See also
Volume 3 pages 53–55

HYDRAULIC: operated by the movement of liquid or by liquid under pressure

One of the German battleships captured at the surrender that ended World War I. Despite its excellent construction, the German fleet was unable to contest effectively the vastly larger Royal Navy.

THE CHEMICAL INDUSTRY

Most of the best-known technical breakthroughs associated with the Industrial Revolution involved machinery such as Arkwright's water frame (see Volume 2) and Watt's steam engine. During the same time that tinkerers and brilliant inventors were perfecting machines, an entirely different group was experimenting with change in a new direction. They were scientists devoted to a branch of science called chemistry, and they were involved in basic research and experimentation with the elements themselves.

THE RISE OF ORGANIC CHEMISTRY

Beginning in the 1820s, a series of landmark discoveries provided the basis for what became the organic chemical industry. Organic chemicals are carbon-based; in other words, they all contain the carbon atom. The organic chemical industry, in turn, had a huge influence on how the modern world developed.

Organic chemistry grew from two main branches: the need to make coke (a hotter-burning form of coal) to produce steel and the search for artificial dyes to color mass-produced textiles. Technicians heated coal to make coke (see Volume 2). The coal, in turn, gave off gases that could be collected and used. But exactly how to do this was not known. The search for dyes flowed from the fact that both clothing designers and consumers wanted a greater selection of colors for their clothes. It was also important that the colors be bright and not fade.

In 1856 the chemist William Perkin was trying to synthesize, or artificially produce, **coal tar.** Coal tar was one of the byproducts of making coke. As was the case with many chemical discoveries, while performing his research, he accidently produced something else, the first coal-tar dye. It was a purple dye that took the French name mauve. Until 1856 all dyes used to color textiles had come from natural substances such as roots and vegetables. Perkin's research helped launch a new era of synthetic, or artificial, dyes. In 1857 he established a manufacturing plant near London, and the synthetic dye-manufacturing industry was born. Later

Long before people understood much about chemistry, it held a fascination for those with inquiring minds and a willingness to experiment.

COAL TAR: a thick, black liquid distilled from coal

Indigo, a plant from which blue dye is made, grows only in a warm climate. Growing indigo and making the dye both required great care. When the indigo plant flowered, it was harvested, and the leaves and stems were crushed in a vat. The indigo was left to ferment and then beaten until flakes of blue dye formed. The dye then was allowed to settle to the bottom of the vat, and the liquid drained off. The flakes were pressed into cakes and sun-dried. The timing of the harvest and the time that fermentation was stopped were both critical to the quality of the dye's color. One mistake could ruin the whole year. Such unpredictability made the supply of natural dyes too unreliable for the modern textile industry.

Perkin also made discoveries that started the artificial perfume and flavoring industries.

While Perkin had more or less stumbled onto a synthetic dye, in contrast, the manufacture of an affordable and easy to produce azo dye (so called because of the presence of nitrogen, called azote by chemists) came from purposeful investigation. The rapidly expanding textile industry had created enormous demand for dyes to color woven materials. People doubted that natural dyes could meet the demand. In 1869 one British and two German chemists, working separately, sought an artificial replacement for the natural dye called madder. They first studied the chemical structure of the natural dye and then tried to make a substitute. Their effort led to the creation of alizarin, the first successful, planned synthesis of an artificial dye.

The goal of the scientists was to make dyes with commercial value. For example, silk could be highly colored with **aniline** dyes, and that appealed to imaginative French designers who set the world's fashion standards. But organic chemistry was still a new field, and the scientists were conducting experiments with chemicals that they did not fully understand. In one early British research facility the shed where investigations with nitrogen took place was called "the shooting gallery" because of the frequency of accidental explosions!

Regardless of the dangers, organic chemistry flourished in European laboratories as researchers discovered and perfected

ANILINE: a liquid base for dyes, at one time extracted from the indigo plant, but now synthesized from nitrobenzene, a coal tar product

new dyes. The new dyes could penetrate various types of fibers and remain fixed to these fibers even after being washed. At the same time, chemists gained a better understanding of the chemicals associated with coal tar, coal gas, and petroleum.

By the late 1860s German scientists had established themselves as world leaders in organic chemistry, and German production of dyes and the chemicals that made dyes (called dyestuffs) rose dramatically. By the end of 1880 German dyestuffs accounted for half the world market, and by 1900 an overwhelming 90 percent. The actual dominance was even greater because German-run affiliates in other countries commonly controlled foreign output of dyestuffs. For example, in France only one major dyestuff plant was French owned and managed, while six were controlled by Germans. In the words of the *Cambridge Economic History of Europe*, this dominance "was Imperial Germany's greatest industrial achievement."

THE SOLVAY PROCESS: THE RISE OF INORGANIC CHEMISTRY

Applying dyes to fabrics was once a labor-intensive task. An eighteenth-century European dyeing workshop.

Around 1860 worldwide demand increased dramatically for alkali, which in its most common form is called bleaching powder. Industrial uses included whitening paper while it was made and the bleaching of textiles; households also needed

ERNEST SOLVAY

Ernest Solvay was born in a small village near Brussels, Belgium, in 1838. After completing school, he went to work at his father's salt-manufacturing business. At age 21 he joined his uncle, who was director of a gasworks near Brussels. A gasworks produced large amounts of ammonia as a waste byproduct, and there Solvay began working on a commercial process to recover ammonia from sodium carbonate (soda ash).

A French chemist had identified the chemical reaction involved in the ammonia-soda process back in 1811, but Solvay was apparently unaware of it. Solvay invented his own process, called "the Solvay carbonating tower." In 1863 he and his brother formed their own company and built a factory to produce ammonia soda. Production began in 1865, but many technical obstacles remained. By the mid-1870s Solvay's process became usable in practice, and over the next several decades his technique outcompeted the Leblanc process and made Solvay a rich man. He spent much of his wealth on philanthropic causes, especially the founding of international scientific institutes. The Solvay conferences on physics provided a key forum for the development of ground-breaking theories in physics and chemistry.

alkalis for soap. The demand was so high that Great Britain (the world leader in production) tripled its production of soda ash, used to make alkalis, between 1852 and 1878.

All nations used the Leblanc process (see Volume 3) to make alkali. When originally developed, it had been a fine technological breakthrough, but it yielded several undesirable byproducts, including hydrochloric acid gas and vast quantities of a smelly mud that required disposal somewhere. The pollution problem was so severe that in 1863 the British Parliament passed the Alkali Works Act, which required a 95 percent reduction in hydrochloric acid gas emissions.

An alternative to the Leblanc process relied on a chemical reaction that produced sodium bicarbonate and ammonium chloride as byproducts. This reaction did not involve carbon and thus was an inorganic (without carbon) process rather than an organic (carbon-based) process. From a chemical standpoint the alternative reaction was much more efficient. From a manufacturing standpoint it was even better because it did not consume so much raw material or generate so much waste.

Scientists understood what they wanted to do, but they did not know how to do it. Although many tried, and vast sums were spent, no one could find a commercially useful process. In the 1860s a 21-year-old Belgian named Ernest Solvay set his mind to the challenge.

After several disappointments Solvay perfected what became known as "the Solvay process." The Solvay process recovered ammonia from ammonium chloride in a commercially successful operation. By the mid-1870s Solvay alkalis undersold Leblanc alkalis by 20 percent. What followed was like the competition between the British and German steel industries, with English manufacturers clinging to the Leblanc process because they had invested so much in it, while German manufacturers widely adopted the Solvay technique. Additional technical improvements in the Solvay technique during the 1890s marked its decisive triumph over the Leblanc process. For the first time since the start of the Industrial Revolution Great Britain's production from the once great Leblanc industry declined. By 1920—less than 100 years after Great Britain had begun making bleaching powder using the Leblanc process—the last facility closed.

Chemistry:
See also
Volume 2 pages 41–43

The search for dyes and development of the Solvay process were only two activities among many in the chemistry industry. Researchers investigated numerous other areas, including cellulose, the major solid component of natural plants, which led to the development of the powerful explosive nitrocellulose as well as lacquers, photographic plates, artificial fibers, and the first modern plastic (celluloid) in 1868. Indeed, organic chemistry had nearly limitless possibilities. By the end of the 1860s an era of scientific experimentation for specific purposes had begun, and the world would never again be the same.

The rise of the chemical industry was something extraordinary. It marked the birth of an entirely new industry that dramatically changed peoples' lives. Ahead lay a future in which chemists worked with nature's smallest building blocks to manufacture everything from medicines and modern pharmaceuticals to fuels and building materials. Where once they had labored to produce artificial dyes to color natural fibers, chemists progressed to creating the fibers themselves, such as nylon and rayon.

The rise of the chemical industry also revealed something else. England had been the birthplace of the Industrial Revolution. But its dyestuff industry failed to keep pace with that of Germany because of weaker technical training and education, a lack of government involvement, and an absence of vision about future possibilities. Although it was not apparent at the time, Great Britain was losing the industrial spirit that had propelled it to the leading position among industrial powers.

The first Solvay process alkali plant in the United States began operating at Syracuse, New York, in 1882.

A DATELINE OF MAJOR EVENTS DURING THE INDUSTRIAL REVOLUTION

BEFORE 1750	1760	1770	1780

REVOLUTIONS IN INDUSTRY AND TECHNOLOGY

1619: English settlers establish the first iron works in colonial America, near Jamestown, Virginia.

1689: Thomas Savery (England) patents the first design for a steam engine.

1709: Englishman Abraham Darby uses coke instead of coal to fuel his blast furnace.

1712: Englishman Thomas Newcomen builds the first working steam engine.

1717: Thomas Lombe establishes a silk-throwing factory in England.

1720: The first Newcomen steam engine on the Continent is installed at a Belgian coal mine.

1733: James Kay (England) invents the flying shuttle.

1742: Benjamin Huntsman begins making crucible steel in England.

1756: The first American coal mine opens.

1764: In England James Hargreaves invents the spinning jenny.

1769: Englishman Richard Arkwright patents his spinning machine, called a water frame.

James Watt of Scotland patents an improved steam engine design.

Josiah Wedgwood (England) opens his Etruria pottery works.

1771: An industrial spy smuggles drawings of the spinning jenny from England to France.

1774: John Wilkinson (England) builds machines for boring cannon cylinders.

1775: Arkwright patents carding, drawing, and roving machines.

In an attempt to end dependence on British textiles American revolutionaries open a spinning mill in Philadelphia using a smuggled spinning-jenny design.

1777: Oliver Evans (U.S.) invents a card-making machine.

1778: John Smeaton (England) introduces cast iron gearing to transfer power from waterwheels to machinery.

The water closet (indoor toilet) is invented in England.

1779: Englishman Samuel Crompton develops the spinning mule.

1783: Englishman Thomas Bell invents a copper cylinder to print patterns on fabrics.

1784: Englishman Henry Cort invents improved rollers for rolling mills and the puddling process for refining pig iron.

Frenchman Claude Berthollet discovers that chlorine can be used as a bleach.

The ironworks at Le Creusot use France's first rotary steam engine to power its hammers, as well as using the Continent's first coke-fired blast furnace.

1785: Englishman Edmund Cartwright invents the power loom.

1788: The first steam engine is imported into Germany.

REVOLUTIONS IN TRANSPORTATION AND COMMUNICATION

1757: The first canal is built in England.

Locks on an English canal

1785: The first canal is built in the United States, at Richmond, Virginia.

1787: John Fitch and James Rumsey (U.S.) each succeed in launching a working steamboat.

SOCIAL REVOLUTIONS

1723: Britain passes an act to allow the establishment of workhouses for the poor.

1750: The enclosure of common land gains momentum in Britain.

1776: Scottish professor Adam Smith publishes *The Wealth of Nations*, which promotes laissez-faire capitalism.

The workhouse

INTERNATIONAL RELATIONS

Continental Army in winter quarters at Valley Forge

1775 –1783: The American Revolution. Thirteen colonies win their independence from Great Britain and form a new nation, the United States of America.

1789–1793: The French Revolution leads to abolition of the monarchy and execution of the king and queen. Mass executions follow during the Reign of Terror, 1793–1794.

1790	1800	1810	1820

1790: English textile producer Samuel Slater begins setting up America's first successful textile factory in Pawtucket, Rhode Island.

Jacob Perkins (U.S.) invents a machine capable of mass-producing nails.

1791: French chemist Nicholas Leblanc invents a soda-making process.

1793: Eli Whitney (U.S.) invents a cotton gin.

1794: Germany's first coke-fired blast furnace is built.

The first German cotton spinning mill installs Arkwright's water frame.

1798: Eli Whitney devises a system for using power-driven machinery to produce interchangeable parts, the model for the "American System" of manufacture.

Wool-spinning mills are built in Belgium using machinery smuggled out of England.

A cylindrical papermaking machine is invented in England.

1801: American inventor Oliver Evans builds the first working high-pressure steam engine and uses it to power a mill.

Joseph-Marie Jacquard (France) invents a loom that uses punch cards to produce patterned fabrics.

A cotton-spinning factory based on British machinery opens in Belgium.

The first cotton-spinning mill in Switzerland begins operation.

Austria establishes the Continent's largest cotton-spinning mill.

1802: In England William Murdock uses coal gas to light an entire factory.

Richard Trevithick builds a high-pressure steam engine in England.

1807: British businessmen open an industrial complex in Belgium that includes machine manufacture, coal mining, and iron production.

1808: Russia's first spinning mill begins production in Moscow.

1810: Henry Maudslay (England) invents the precision lathe.

1816: Steam power is used for the first time in an American paper mill.

English scientist Humphry Davy invents a safety lamp for coal miners in England.

1817: The French iron industry's first puddling works and rolling mills are established.

1819: Thomas Blanchard (U.S.) invents a gunstock-turning lathe, which permits production of standardized parts.

A turning lathe

1821: Massachusetts businessmen begin developing Lowell as a site for textile mills.

1822: Power looms are introduced in French factories.

1820s: Spinning mills begin operation in Sweden.

Steam power is first used in Czech industry.

1827: A water-driven turbine is invented in France.

1794: The 66-mile Philadelphia and Lancaster turnpike begins operation.

Along an American Highway

1802: In England Richard Trevithick builds his first steam locomotive.

1807: Robert Fulton launches the Clermont, the first commercially successful steamboat, on the Hudson River in New York.

1811: Robert Fulton and his partner launch the first steamboat on the Mississippi River.

Construction begins on the Cumberland Road (later renamed the National Road) from Baltimore, Maryland, to Wheeling, Virginia.

1815: In England John McAdam develops an improved technique for surfacing roads.

1819: The first steamship crosses the Atlantic Ocean.

1825: The 363-mile Erie Canal is completed in America.

In England the first passenger railroad, the Stockton and Darlington Railway, begins operation.

1826: The 2-mile horse-drawn Granite Railroad in Massachusetts becomes the first American railroad.

1790: First American patent law passed.

Philadelphia begins building a public water system.

1798: Robert Owen takes over the New Lanark mills and begins implementing his progressive ideas.

1800: Parliament prohibits most labor union activity.

1802: Parliament passes a law limiting the working hours of poor children and orphans.

1811–1816: Luddite rioters destroy textile machinery in England.

1819: Parliament extends legal protection to all child laborers.

British cavalry fire at demonstrators demanding voting reform in Manchester, killing 11 and wounding hundreds, including women and children.

1827: Carpenters organize the first national trade union in Britain.

18th–century carpenter

1799: Napoleon Bonaparte seizes control of France's government.

1792–1815: The Napoleonic Wars involve most of Europe, Great Britain, and Russia. France occupies many of its neighboring nations, reorganizes their governments, and changes their borders.

1812–1815: War between the United States and Great Britain disrupts America's foreign trade and spurs the development of American industry.

A DATELINE OF MAJOR EVENTS DURING THE INDUSTRIAL REVOLUTION

	1830	1840	1850	1860
REVOLUTIONS IN INDUSTRY AND TECHNOLOGY	1830: Switzerland's first weaving mill established. 1831: British researcher Michael Faraday builds an electric generator. American inventor Cyrus McCormick builds a horse-drawn mechanical reaper. 1834: Bulgaria's first textile factory is built. 1835: Samuel Colt (U.S)invents the Colt revolver. The first steam engine is used to power a paper mill in Croatia. 1836: The first Hungarian steam mill, the Pest Rolling Mill company, begins using steam power to process grain. 1837: The first successful coke-fired blast furnace in the United States begins operation.	American blacksmith John Deere introduces the first steel plow. 1842: Britain lifts restrictions on exporting textile machinery.  Making Bessemer steel	1849: The California Gold Rush begins. 1850: Swedish sawmills begin using steam power. 1851: The Great Exhibition opens at the Crystal Palace in London. William Kelly of Kentucky invents a process for converting pig iron to steel. 1852: Hydraulic mining is introduced in the American West. 1853: The first cotton-spinning mill opens in India. 1856: William Perkin (England) synthesizes the first coal tar dye. Henry Bessemer (England) announces his process for converting pig iron to steel. Isaac Singer (U.S.) introduces the sewing machine.	1859: Edwin Drake successfully drills for oil in Pennsylvania. 1863: Ernest Solvay of Belgium begins working on a process to recover ammonia from soda ash in order to produce bleaching powder. 1864: Switzerland's first major chemical company is established. The Siemens-Martin open-hearth steelmaking process is perfected in France. 1865: The first oil pipeline opens in America. The rotary web press is invented in America, permitting printing on both sides of the paper. 1866: U.S. government surveyors discover the largest-known deposit of iron ore in the world in the Mesabi Range of northern Minnesota.
REVOLUTIONS IN TRANSPORTATION AND COMMUNICATION	1830: The first locomotive-powered railroad to offer regular service begins operating in South Carolina. The opening of the Liverpool and Manchester Railway marks the beginning of the British railroad boom. 1833: The 60-mile Camden and Amboy Railroad of New Jersey is completed. 1835: Construction begins on Germany's first railroad.	1836: First railroad built in Russia. 1843: Tunnel completed under the Thames River, London, England, the world's first to be bored through soft clay under a riverbed. 1844: Samuel Morse (U.S.) sends the first message via his invention, the telegraph. The nation's first steam-powered sawmill begins operation on the West Coast.	1846: First railroad built in Hungary. 1853: The first railway is completed in India. 1854: Americans complete the Moscow-St. Petersburg railroad line. 1855: Switzerland's first railroad opens.	1859: In France Etienne Lenoir invents an internal combustion engine. 1860–1861: The Pony Express, a system of relay riders, carries mail to and from America's West Coast. 1866: The transatlantic telegraph cable is completed. Congress authorizes construction of a transcontinental telegraph line. 1869: The tracks of two railroad companies meet at Promontory, Utah, to complete America's first transcontinental railroad
SOCIAL REVOLUTIONS	1833: Parliament passes the Factory Act to protect children working in textile factories. 1836–1842: The English Chartist movement demands Parliamentary reform, but its petitions are rejected by Parliament. 1838: The U.S. Congress passes a law regulating steamboat boiler safety, the first attempt by the federal government to regulate private behavior in the interest of public safety.	1842: Parliament bans the employment of children and women underground in mines. 1845: Russia bans strikes. 1847: A new British Factory Act limits working hours to 10 hours a day or 58 hours a week for children aged 13 to 18 and for women. 1848: Marx and Engels coauthor the Communist Manifesto.	1854: In England Charles Dickens publishes *Hard Times*, a novel based on his childhood as a factory worker. 1857: Brooklyn, New York, builds a city wastewater system.	1860–1910: More than 20 million Europeans emigrate to the United States. 1866: National Labor Union forms in the United States. 1869: Knights of Labor forms in the United States. Founding of the Great Atlantic and Pacific Tea Company (A&P) in the U.S.
INTERNATIONAL RELATIONS	1839–1842: Great Britain defeats China in a war and forces it to open several ports to trade.	1847: Austro-Hungary occupies Italy. 1848: Failed revolutions take place in France, Germany, and Austro-Hungary. Serfdom ends in Austro-Hungary.	1853: The American naval officer Commodore Matthew Perry arrives in Japan. 1853–1856: France, Britain, and Turkey defeat Russia in the Crimean War. 1858: Great Britain takes control of India, retaining it until 1947.	1861–1865: The American Civil War brings about the end of slavery in the United States and disrupts raw cotton supplies for U.S. and foreign cotton mills. 1867: Britain gains control of parts of Malaysia. Malaysia is a British colony from 1890 to 1957.

1870	1880	1890	1900

1860s: Agricultural machinery introduced in Hungary.

1870: John D. Rockefeller establishes the Standard Oil Company (U.S.).

1873: The Bethlehem Steel Company begins operation in Pennsylvania.

1875: The first modern iron and steel works opens in India.

Investment in the Japan's cotton industry booms.

1876: Philadelphia hosts the Centennial Exposition.

1877: Hungary installs its first electrical system.

1879: Charles Brush builds the nation's first arc-lighting system in San Francisco.

Thomas Edison (U.S.) develops the first practical incandescent light bulb.

1870s: Japan introduces mechanical silk-reeling.

1882: In New York City the Edison Electric Illuminating Company begins operating the world's first centralized electrical generating station.

1884: The U.S. Circuit Court bans hydraulic mining.

George Westinghouse (U.S.) founds Westinghouse Electric Company.

English engineer Charles Parsons develops a steam turbine.

1885: The introduction of band saws makes American lumbering more efficient.

German inventor Carl Benz builds a self-propelled vehicle powered by a single cylinder gas engine with electric ignition.

1887: An English power plant is the first to use steam turbines to generate electricity.

1888: Nikola Tesla (U.S.) invents an alternating current electric motor.

1894: An American cotton mill becomes the first factory ever built to rely entirely on electric power.

1895: George Westinghouse builds the world's first generating plant designed to transmit power over longer distances—a hydroelectric plant at Niagara Falls to transmit alternating current some 20 miles to consumers in Buffalo, New York.

1901: The United States Steel Corporation is formed by a merger of several American companies.

Japan opens its first major iron and steel works.

1929: The U.S.S.R. begins implementing its first Five-Year Plan, which places nationwide industrial development under central government control.

Power generators at Edison Electric

1875: Japan builds its first railway.

1876: In the U.S. Alexander Graham Bell invents the telephone.

German inventor Nikolaus Otto produces a practical gasoline engine.

1870s: Sweden's railroad boom.

1883: Brooklyn Bridge completed.

1885: Germans Gottlieb Daimler and Wilhelm Maybach build the world's first motorcycle.

1886: Daimler and Maybach invent the carburetor, the device that efficiently mixes fuel and air in internal combustion engines

1888: The first electric urban streetcar system begins operation in Richmond, Virginia.

1893: American brothers Charles and J. Frank Duryea build a working gasoline-powered automobile.

1896: Henry Ford builds a demonstration car powered by an internal combustion engine.

1896–1904: Russia builds the Manchurian railway in China.

1903: Henry Ford establishes Ford Motor Company.

1904: New York City subway system opens.

Trans-Siberian Railroad completed.

1908: William Durant, maker of horse-drawn carriages, forms the General Motors Company.

1909: Ford introduces the Model T automobile.

1870: Parliament passes a law to provide free schooling for poor children.

1872: France bans the International Working Men's Association.

1874: France applies its child labor laws to all industrial establishments and provides for inspectors to enforce the laws.

1877: Wage cuts set off the Great Railroad Strike in West Virginia, and the strike spreads across the country. Federal troops kill 35 strikers.

1880: Parliament makes school attendance compulsory for children between the ages of 5 and 10.

1881: India passes a factory law limiting child employment.

1884: Germany passes a law requiring employers to provide insurance against workplace accidents.

1886: American Federation of Labor forms.

1887: U.S. Interstate Commerce Act passed to regulate railroad freight charges.

1890: The U.S. government outlaws monopolies with passage of the Sherman Antitrust Act.

1892: Workers strike at Carnegie Steel in Homestead, Pennsylvania, in response to wage cuts. An armed confrontation results in 12 deaths.

1894: The Pullman strike, called in response to wage cuts, halts American railroad traffic. A confrontation with 2,000 federal troops kills 12 strikers in Chicago.

1900: Japan passes a law to limit union activity.

1902: The United Mine Workers calls a nationwide strike against coal mines, demanding eight-hour workdays and higher wages.

1903: Socialists organize the Russian Social Democratic Workers Party.

1931: Japan passes a law to limit working hours for women and children in textile factories.

1870: The city-states of Italy unify to form one nation.

1871: Parisians declare self-government in the city but are defeated by government forces.

Prussia and the other German states unify to form the German Empire.

1877–1878: War between Russia and Turkey. Bulgaria gains independence from Turkey.

1900–1901: A popular uprising supported by the Chinese government seeks to eject all foreigners from China.

1917: Russian Revolution

1929: A worldwide economic depression begins.

SCIENTISTS AND INVENTORS

HENRY BESSEMER: 1813–1898; born in England. Aside from his steelmaking process, Bessemer has a wide variety of inventions to his credit. He made improvements to typesetting machinery, formulated a gold-colored powder to tint paint, and invented an artillery shell, a solar furnace, and a telescope. His skill as an inventor brought him varied honors, including a knighthood, and a steelmaking town in Alabama named after him. In 1866 Bessemer formed a steelmaking company with his former competitor, William Kelly, the American who had invented a similar process.

PERCY GILCHRIST: 1851–1935; born in England. While working as a chemist at a large iron works, Gilchrist collaborated with his cousin, Sidney Gilchrist Thomas, to develop and test a new steelmaking process.

WILLIAM KELLY: 1811–1888; born in Kentucky. Kelly was a partner in a merchandise shipping company when he decided to buy an iron works with his brother. As the land around the iron works ran out of trees, Kelly looked for a way to use air to heat and refine pig iron more efficiently. His relatives thought he was losing his mind and sent him to a doctor, but the doctor saw that Kelly's idea made sense. Kelly developed his process during the 1850s but failed to patent it, and Bessemer patented a similar process in Great Britain and the United States. After forming competing steelmaking companies in America, Bessemer and Kelly joined forces in 1866.

PIERRE MARTIN: 1824–1915; born in France. Martin, an engineer, acquired a license to build the open hearth furnace developed by the Siemens brothers. In 1864 Martin devised a method for producing high-quality steel in the open hearth furnace. Although steelmakers widely used his process, Martin lost most of his money in lawsuits over his patent. Only in his old age did Martin receive honors and monetary rewards for his invention.

CHARLES PARSONS: 1854–1931; born in England. While employed by an engine works, Parsons invented the steam turbine. A few years later he established his own facility. His turbine served to generate electricity and to propel ships. He also invented a reducing gear to efficiently link the turbine with a ship's propeller. He received many honors, including a knighthood.

WILLIAM PERKIN: 1838–1907; born in England. Perkin began studying chemistry at the age of 15. He worked in the lab of the noted German chemist August Wilhelm von Hofmann. While still a teenager, Perkin discovered and began producing synthetic dyes. After a period of manufacturing dyes, perfumes, and artificial flavorings, Perkin left the business of manufacturing and turned to pure research. He was knighted in 1906.

FREDERICK SIEMENS: 1826–1904, born in Germany as August Friedrich Siemens. As a young man, Frederick settled in London, where he lived and worked with his brother William. By 1856 Frederick Siemens invented the regenerative open hearth furnace, based on the concept of reusing heat from waste gases.

WILLIAM SIEMENS: 1823–1883; born in Germany as Karl Wilhelm Siemens. Siemens received his education from private tutors before attending classes in chemistry and physics. He then became an apprentice in a steam engine factory. Siemens emigrated to England in 1844, hoping to make his living as an inventor. In 1851 he began earning a substantial sum for his invention of a water meter. In 1858 he married a British woman and became a British citizen. Working with a concept developed by his brother Frederick, Siemens patented the open hearth furnace in 1861. He also invented an improved arc light and built an electric railway. Siemens became wealthy and received many honors, including a knighthood.

ERNEST SOLVAY: 1838–1922; born in Belgium. At the age of 21, Solvay began working on a more efficient process for producing soda ash, an ingredient of soap and bleach. (See page 60 of this volume for more about Solvay.)

SIDNEY GILCHRIST THOMAS: 1850–1885; born in England. Thomas was about to enter medical school when his father's death forced him to change his plans and go to work. While working as a court clerk, he studied chemistry and metallurgy in his spare time. His cousin, Percy Gilchrist, who worked at an iron works, provided a place where he could test his idea for a new steelmaking process. Income from the 1879 patent for his basic steel process permitted Thomas to quit his job and pursue his scientific interests. Sadly, he lived only a few more years.

GLOSSARY

ANILINE: a liquid base for dyes, at one time extracted from the indigo plant, but now synthesized from nitrobenzene, a coal tar product

BLAST FURNACE: a tall furnace that uses a blast of air to generate intense heat capable of melting iron and processing it into a purer form

BURLAP: a coarse fabric woven from jute and used to make large sacks

BYPRODUCT: something produced during the process of making another product

CAPITAL: money or property used in operating a business

CARBON: a chemical element found in all organic compounds and many inorganic compounds

CASTE: rigid class system based on the family of birth; in India members of one caste may not associate with members of another.

COAL TAR: a thick, black liquid distilled from coal

COASTING: shipping along the coast of a nation

COMMODITY: anything that is bought and sold

COTTAGE INDUSTRY: manufacturing goods at home

CRUCIBLE: a container, treated to withstand extreme heat, used for melting a material such as metal

DEPRESSION: decrease in business activity, accompanied by unemployment and lower prices and earnings

DUCTILE: the property of being pliant and flexible, able to be stretched thin without breaking

ENTREPRENEUR: one who establishes and manages a business

FEUDAL: of the medieval system under which serfs worked on land held by a lord and gave part of their produce to the lord

FORGE: a site where iron is heated in a fire and shaped by hammering

GENERATOR: an engine that converts mechanical energy, such as flowing water, to electrical energy

HEMATITE: a type of iron ore valued for its high iron content; its name comes from the Greek word for blood because of its reddish color

HORSEPOWER: a unit of engine power believed to be equivalent to the power of a horse

HYDRAULIC: operated by the movement of liquid or by liquid under pressure

INDIGO: a blue dye or the plant from which it is made

INFRASTRUCTURE: underlying support, usually referring to the roads and other services provided to a community

JUTE: a coarse fiber made from a plant that grows in Asia

KINETIC: producing or produced by motion

MADDER: a natural red dye made from the roots of the madder plant or the synthetic red dye made from coal tar

MONOPOLY: exclusive right to control the purchase and sale of specific goods or services

MUSLIN: a fine cotton cloth made in India

OPEN HEARTH FURNACE: a furnace that uses the waste gases generated while heating pig iron to heat a honeycomb of bricks, making it possible to heat iron to a higher temperature and remove more impurities

ORGANIC CHEMISTRY: the branch of chemistry dealing with chemical compounds containing carbon

PEASANT: rural dweller and farm worker

PIG IRON: the product created by smelting iron ore in a furnace

PUDDLING: a process for converting pig iron to wrought iron by melting and stirring it

ROLLING MILL: a mill that uses heavy rollers to form molten iron or steel into sheets or rails

SAMURAI: an aristocratic class of Japanese warriors that, allied with noblemen, controlled Japanese local government from the twelfth century until the mid-1800s

SHOGUNS: Japanese military governors who held the actual power in Japan, forcing the emperor into a merely symbolic role

SLAG: the waste product produced while smelting metal

SMELTING: melting metal ore to extract the pure metal

STEAM ENGINE: an engine that uses steam under pressure to produce power. In the most basic form of steam engine steam enters a cylinder and is then compressed with a piston.

STEEL: strong metal made by combining iron with small amounts of carbon or other substances

SUBSISTENCE: production of just enough to survive

TARIFF: tax on imports; duty

TURBINE: a wheel-shaped engine driven by steam or water pressure on its curved spokes

UNDERWRITE: to make an agreement undertaking to accept responsibility or make payment for a third party

WROUGHT IRON: iron after the removal of most impurities. Wrought iron is strong but able to be shaped by hammering.

ADDITIONAL RESOURCES

BOOKS:

Bland, Celia. *The Mechanical Age: The Industrial Revolution in England*. New York: Facts on File, 1995.

Bolitho, Harold. *Meiji Japan*. New York: Cambridge University Press, 1977.

Bridgman, Roger. *Inventions and Discoveries*. London: Dorling-Kindersley Publishing, 2002.

Ebrey, Patricia Buckley. *The Cambridge Illustrated History of China*. New York: Cambridge University Press, 1996.

Ingpen, Robert, Robert R. Wilkinson, and Philip Wilkinson. *Encyclopedia of Ideas That Changed the World*. New York: Viking, 1993.

Lines, Clifford. *Companion to the Industrial Revolution*. New York: Facts on File, 1990

WEBSITES:

http://academic.reed.edu/formosa
Images from 19th century Taiwan, once a province of China

http://albumen.stanford.edu/gallery/gadd/
Photographs taken in Meiji-era Japan

http://vlib.iue.it/history/index.html
Virtual Library-History Central Catalogue
Links to maps, biographies, and essays about the countries listed in the index

SET INDEX

Bold numbers refer to volumes

PICTURE CREDITS

Colonial Williamsburg Foundation: 57, 62 right; Denis Diderot, *Encyclopedie ou dictionnaire raisonné des Sciences, des arts et des metiers*, 1765: 58, 59; *Frank Leslie's Illustrated Historical Register of the Centennial Exposition, 1876*: 22, 51; Ironbridge Gorge Museum Trust: 55, 62 top left; National Archives: 54, 63 left, 65; National Museum of American History, Smithsonian Institution: 63 top right; National Park Service, Artist, L. Kenneth Townsend: 48, 52 top, 53 top; Collection of the New York Historical Society: 25 top (acc. # 1946.82); All other pictures, including the cover picture, are from the Library of Congress.